LG -3.2 -0.5pts

Autobiographies You Never
Thought You'd Read

THE
LOCH NESS
MONSTER

Catherine Chambers

heinemann
raintree

© 2016 Heinemann-Raintree
an imprint of Capstone Global Library, LLC
Chicago, Illinois

To contact Capstone Global Library please call 800-747-4992, or visit our web site www.capstonepub.com

Edited by Linda Staniford
Designed by Steve Mead
Original illustrations © Capstone Global Library Ltd 2015
Illustrated by Lois Billau - Advocate Art
Production by Victoria Fitzgerald
Originated by Capstone Global Library
Printed and bound in China by Leo Paper Products

19 18 17 16 15
10 9 8 7 6 5 4 3 2 1

Library of Congress Cataloging-in-Publication Data
Chambers, Catherine, 1954- author.
  The Loch Ness Monster / Catherine Chambers.
      pages cm.—(Autobiographies you never thought you'd read)
  Includes bibliographical references and index.
  ISBN 978-1-4109-7962-9 (hb)—ISBN 978-1-4109-7967-4 (pb)—ISBN 978-1-4109-7977-3 (ebook) 1. Loch Ness monster—Juvenile literature. 2. Ness, Loch (Scotland)—Juvenile literature. I. Title.
  QL89.2.L6C5 2006
  001.944—dc23   2015000252

Acknowledgments
Every effort has been made to contact copyright holders of material reproduced in this book. Any omissions will be rectified in subsequent printings if notice is given to the publisher.

Contents

Some words are shown in bold, **like this**. You can find out what they mean by looking in the glossary.

Who Am I?
Where Do I Live?

My name is Nessie. I live in a very deep **freshwater** lake called **Loch** Ness, in Scotland.

Some people think I'm a monster. That's why I'm known as the Loch Ness Monster.

What Do I Look Like?

I am huge, with a slippery skin. My neck and tail are long and graceful. My back arches into a large hump, or maybe two or three!

DID YOU KNOW?

Loch Ness is 22 miles (36 km) long. In places, it is 754 feet (230 meters) deep and very dark. Some people think it is hard to spot Nessie because she hides at the bottom.

Where Do I Come From?

I think I was born here in Scotland. It's hard to remember since it was so long ago, maybe even millions of years in the past. Some people say I come from **prehistoric** times.

DID YOU KNOW?

A long-necked prehistoric **reptile** called a **plesiosaur** lived from about 205 million years ago. Is Nessie like this?

What Was My Childhood Like?

When I was very young, the **loch** shook a lot from terrifying earth tremors. The water was very warm.

DID YOU KNOW?

Loch Ness was formed about 500 million years ago. Water filled up a huge crack that was created by the earth tremors.

These days, the loch still shakes a little. The water is not as warm as it used to be, but it doesn't freeze over in winter.

Who Spotted Me First?

People who lived in Scotland in the **Bronze** and Iron Ages might have spotted me first. They spoke of water horses with long necks. That sounds like me, don't you think?

Then the **Vikings** invaded and said they saw water horses, too. So maybe I'm a water horse, and what people had seen before were my relatives.

A Saint Says I'm a Monster!

There is an old story about me that tells of a holy man named Saint Columba. He said I'd killed a human! Huh? So Columba rowed a boat to the middle of the **loch**. He called out, "Don't you ever kill anyone again!"

DID YOU KNOW?

The story of Saint Columba was first written down 100 years later by a monk called Saint Adamnan.

What Do I Eat?

I really don't eat humans. I can catch plenty of tasty salmon and eels. I'd also like to try some healthy green leaves. But the **loch** is so deep and dark that water plants can't grow easily.

Peat soil from around the loch slips into the water and makes it murky.

My Brave Brush with Humans

I was careful not to show myself much for many **centuries**. But in the 1930s, a road was built all around my lovely **loch**. Tourists came to admire this beautiful natural spot.

Then one day in April 1933, I popped up my head to take a look at the people. Instead, I found they were all looking at ME!

I panicked and rolled around in the water. Two tourists hurried off to tell the whole world what they had seen. All went quiet. But that winter, I rose to the surface of the lake and heard a "CLICK!" Someone took my picture!

DID YOU KNOW?

Hugh Gray was the man with the camera. The *Daily Sketch* newspaper published his picture.

MYSTERIOUS MONSTER OF.

LOCH NESS

NIGHTMARE SHAPE, BEAST WITH 7 FT. NECK

N. 5,958

WEDNESDAY 6TH DEC. 1933

Daily Sketch

ONE PENNY

My Worst Moment

One day, I saw a lot of boats sailing together in a row. What were they up to? I dived to the bottom for safety.

Then I looked up and watched them moving across the **loch**. I soon felt strong waves of sound hitting me. It was scary.

A Close Shave

I heard later that the boats carried electronic **sonar** units. The sonar sent sound waves across the whole **loch**. That's what hit me!

The waves recorded three lumps in the loch. Was one of them me?

DID YOU KNOW?

The sonar project was called Deepscan. It was led by Adrian Shine from the Loch Ness Project.

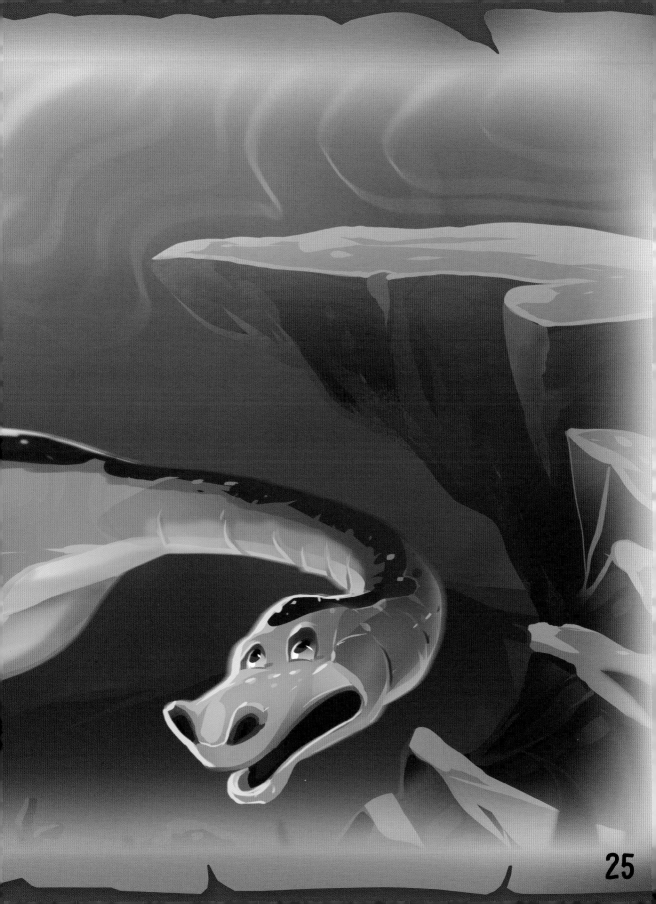

Could I Be Smarter Than Humans?

Well, the people tried again the next day and recorded...nothing. I'm way too smart to let them find me!

Some people have given up. Others say I'm just a big fish! But there are always those who just keep on looking.

DID YOU KNOW?

In 1967, even Britain's Royal Air Force film unit tried to analyze film from **Loch** Ness.

Do I Really Exist?

Of course I exist! But you might never find me. It's hard to see down here. The water is very dark and cloudy.

Divers find the water pressure too heavy for them. I think I'm safe from you all. At least, I hope so!

Glossary

bronze metal used to make tools and weapons from about 4,500 to 3,000 years ago. This period is known as the Bronze Age.

century one hundred years

freshwater water that is not salty like the sea

loch large, deep lake

peat damp soil made of plant material

plesiosaur long-necked prehistoric reptile that swam in the sea

prehistoric time period in human history before there were written records

reptile cold-blooded, egg-laying creature. Crocodiles, snakes, and lizards are reptiles.

sonar sound waves that are pushed out to detect objects or used to communicate underwater

Viking invading forces from Norway about 1,200 years ago

Find Out More

You could find out more about the Loch Ness Monster in other books and on the Internet.

Books

Hile, Lori. *The Loch Ness Monster* (Solving Mysteries with Science). Chicago: Raintree, 2013.
This book explores the stories about the Loch Ness Monster and investigates to see if they might be true.

Schach, David. *The Loch Ness Monster* (Torque: The Unexplained). Minneapolis: Bellwether, 2011.
This book tells more about the Loch Ness Monster.

Sievert, Terri. *The Unsolved Mystery of the Loch Ness Monster* (First Facts: Unexplained Mysteries). N. Mankato, Minn.: Capstone, 2013.
This book explores the mystery of the Loch Ness Monster.

Web sites

Facthound offers a safe, fun way to find Internet sites related to this book. All of the sites on Facthound have been researched by our staff.

Here's all you do:
Visit *www.facthound.com*
Type in this code: 9781410979629

Index